MW01268354

American Legends

by

Cary Kamarat

Here's another perspective on your adopted country. I do hope you enjoy it!

God bless,

CK.

ISBN 978-1-62806-220-5

Library of Congress Control Number 2019940979

Published by Salt Water Media
29 Broad Street, Suite 104
Berlin, MD 21811
www.saltwatermedia.com

Cover photograph and interior photographs
used courtesy of the author who obtained permission
from the Chief of the Nanticoke Indian Association
to photograph the annual powwow.

Dedication

This book is dedicated to the leaders and supporters of the American Indian College Fund, who are actively engaged in leveling the playing field for Native American youth, and guiding all of us who care—who have no choice but to care—in 'paying it forward'.

Acknowledgements

My gratitude and heartfelt thanks go to…

The *Lehaq'temish*, the Lummi People of the Pacific Northwest, who held me enthralled with the energy and magic of the Bone Game and the Sacred Pipe, at my very first powwow, long long ago;

Larry Jackson, former Chief of the Nanticoke Indian Association, for his warm Nanticoke welcome to my first Eastern Shore powwow, and his personal notes on celebration and respect for our Native heritage;

Yankee-of-the-Turtle-Clan, for his tales acquainting me with a living Oral Tradition, as well as to the many other tradition bearers who have shown me how storytelling may be shaped by the teller, the listener, and their moment in time;

The participants in the Pachamama Alliance, who work toward a coming-of-age in our worldview, for the sake of our own and our children's future;

Native American Netroots, and similar online forums devoted to the preservation of American Indian culture and identity;

The Webmasters of *First People: Native American Poems and Prayers*, for accepting my first attempts at exploration of my own acquired, American Indian roots;

Robert Busch, who showed me how "human imagination has wrongly tainted the wolf," providing me with a wealth of information on wolf behaviors and habitats [*The Wolf Almanac*, 2018];

GaWaNi Pony Boy, for helping me to see and understand the legendary bond between horse and rider that has come to us from Native America [*Horse, Follow Closely*, 1998];

And last, but never least: George Cronyn, and a magnificent array of American Indian poets, whose songs and chants introduced me to the spirit, rhythms, language, and forms of Native poetry [*Native American Poetry*, 2006].

Literary circles do not always make kind use of the term *derivative*. Calling a work derivative may imply that it lacks originality and merely rides in on the back of an earlier literary success. *American Legends*, by definition and for better or for worse, is derivative. It is based on Native American legends, or legendary mores, passions, beliefs, and accounts. As American Indian poetry derives from the Native experience and explores a wealth of expression within the parameters of that experience, these poems attempt to explore that adopted America that I have missed out on most of my life.

If I were to uproot now with the intention of settling in another country, I could look forward to new music, new foods, new expressions if not an entirely new language, new values that might interface with and possibly modify my own over time. But as a native-born American of European heritage, I have needed to clear away enough of the dross of our history to allow American Indian culture to become a part of my own personal America.

The retelling of a legend is always a labor of re-creation and adaptation. But original creativity can also emerge through fresh juxtaposition of images and other story elements. The fresh perspective of an appropriately adapted narrative can reveal insights and lend a heightened sense of the legend as metaphor. At times, I have chosen to relate a magical slice of legend rather than offer an exhaustive or definitive retelling. But I have always sought to capture the rhetoric and sensibilities of Native poetry.

In actual Native American poetry, there is no clear and firm distinction between the poem, the song, and the dance. Where one happens, so does the other. In place of meter, there tend to be arrangements of breath groups and repetition of words and phrases similar to some of the language of our Bible. In addition, syllables with no lexical purpose beyond the sheer pleasure of sound may be used to keep the music of language, rhythm, energy and emotion flowing. Anything else may be referred to by some as 'poetic interpretation'. And of course, there is often little separation from elements of the natural environment.

A word about photographs. In my first book, *Travelwalk*, each photo illustrated or provided a thematic context for a given poem. In my second collection, *Out of Delmarva*, photos were meant as individual poems in themselves. In *American Legends*, however, the photography is intended to provide a decorative visual plane of Native American patterns, costume, music and dance, running alongside the verse. In a sense, each picture is a kind of legend in itself. If the reader feels inclined to draw connections with the surrounding poetry, so much the richer.

This has been a learning and growing experience for me—a journey, in the richest sense of the word. I hope that the reader is able to discern some measure of the love that I have poured into the journey.

Table of Contents

Four Spirits

Grandfather of the North, control the power of Rock
that breaks to leave its offspring all around,
that dwells in Winter's ice and snow, in our bodies,
in the clinging tree, and all that here is solid.

Grandmother of the South, control the Fire, and with it
imbue each living fiber with Summer's spirit.
Light corners where your sun-flame is unknown,
And suffer the warring tribes to mature, then grow.

Grandfather of the East, control the Wind, and through it
bring life renewed to knowledge, song, and music.
Springtime belongs to you and all your children,
who consecrate the light of new beginnings.

Grandfather of the West, control the power of Water
to soften the Divine with tears and streams of laughter.
Grant Autumn the death that harbingers rebirth,
and to blood the healing rain that dreams of earth.

Howling Wolf

Lone Wolf that raises the high howling skies
Run the bright trail of the long Milky Way
Run your Wolf Trail and down Northern Lights
From the Spirit World come, cover-the-ground, away.

Cover-the-ground, then rest and let Sleeping Wolf stand
Let the dawn and the scent of Earth fill heart and soul
Once sent to discover the far reaches of land
Cover-the-ground as Creation still dares to unfold.

Human eyes of gold ember turned green in the night
Avatar of the East and of those you adore
Tease the day, pierce the darkness, spawn of worship and fright
Men have begged your forgiveness, men have envied your war.

Wolf-in-the-Water, teach Woman to howl
Howl of joy and of mourning, of alarm wild and deep
In a harmony of discord, cover ground to devour
All of space across prairie and hill green and steep.

Lone-Wolf, when you dream gray and white, red and black
And a memory twists your soft face to a scowl
For the loss of companions of your own rainbow pack
Surely joy that is lost is a reason to howl.

Cover-the-ground, cover-the-ground
Where does the world end?
Cover-the-ground, Lone-Wolf
Cover-the ground.

Light

Kunakwat, lowat, nuchink

Long ago,
the Creator dwelled in silence and peace,
but without Creation.

Then a vision came to bring the unseen:
a sun and stars, a moon and Earth,
good-natured valleys and tender streams;

trees that bloomed as forests,
flowers and grasses that blossomed to crops,
and mighty lands and waters.

Creatures gave and were given birth
to crawl and walk as they grew,
to swim and fly, and fight unto death,

while other beings waxed eternal
in courage, stories, and songs.
And the Creator heard their songs on the wind,

their laughter and tears on the rain,
and was moved to touch the wind and the rain.
But with a touch, the vision was gone.

Once again,
the Creator dwelled in silence and peace,
but without Creation.

And so the Creator said,
Let there be Light....

Messiah

How can I feel the boundaries of my land—
How can I know the limits of my earth—
How can I dance in unison-making harmony—
Messiah

He'e'yo!
He'e'yo!

How can we ever come together now—
How can we rekindle lamps of truth—
How can we know our prophets true or false—
Messiah

He'e'yo!
He'e'yo!

Through body and spirit a shaking of the earth
Fills gourds with ash that dusts the pressing hours—
Barriers cannot heal a vanishing people,
But the child of hope will sleep in the House of Glass.

How can new spirit devour the greed—
How can I know myself without you—
How can I know myself—
Messiah

He'e'yo!
He'e'yo!

19

Mother Corn

Standing tall, rising high
above the earth, your golden hair
silken to the touch, as soft with care
we seek to understand your mystery,
Mother Corn—

Nourish as you lead us on,
rooted now where fathers lay,
guide your children whose futures weigh
heavily upon your history,
Mother Corn—

Aloft above the field, your sigh
beneath the force of crackling wind
has sanctified this journey of womankind
that we must follow, in purpose and song,
Mother Corn—

From sign to sign your trails have gone,
as we sing to the rivers and trees we know,
as we taste our joy in the seed we sow,
our love, our lives, may you prolong them,
Mother Corn.

Old Oraibi

Old Oraibi has no stone
To mark the spot where the land grew small,
When soldiers tore at sons and daughters
And families bowed and broken watched—
    Ahi-yo, Ahi-yo

Old Oraibi has no stone
To build the school of grief where children
Learn the hunger they shall need
To please the soldiers of the dusty flag—
    Ahi-yo, Ahi-yo

Old Oraibi has no stone
For the town crier to rest where he cries,
His messages found beneath pottery shards
Where dark tales stain the dust—
    Ahi-yo

        And so the stranger kicks the dog,
        And so he cripples the faithful horse,
        And so he crushes the Savior-God
        That he has brought to the People of Peace.

Old Oraibi has no stone
To seal the shrines, the fourteen kivas,
Split and charred like Old Oraibi,
Hating themselves, like Old Oraibi—
    Ahi-yo, Ahi-yo

Pony Man
Iyuptála

Our woven locks of windblown mane and feathered hair
attune our interwoven lives to a single flow.
Two souls as one, we fly over sweet and rocky meadows
like the flocks above in focal harmony.
You-of-the-Hunted-Herd and I-of-the-Hunters,
we create as we discover our language of brothers—
Iyuptála: One-with-each-other.

If I taste the waters for you,
then guard the watering place
and watch while you take your fill,
will you catch me when I fall?

If I show you my body's words,
then bring you to sleep in the dry
and soft quiet of family,
will you share my trust, my breath?

If I hand you the pasture, hand-graze
with you in your world, just to know it,
may I rest my eyes on your brow
when the stream of faith overflows?

What you are is the smallest part of Who you are—
how you play and rest, how you watch and are watched,
how you celebrate with me the new spring grass.
And having chased the sun around the world,
You-of-the-Hunted-Herd and I-of-the-Hunters
will long discover, as we create, our language of brothers—
Iyuptála: One-with-each-other.

Stepping Stones

In the order of Creation lie the stones,
stepping stones that join one life to lives,
crossing the trampled earth from sun to sun
like a reflexion in the skin of humankind.

No darkening descent from lofty slopes,
nor loss to the depths of wrong, to the black ravine.
No rising to a realm of worthier fire,
nor less the worth of one's own share of fire:

All color quickens in the light of night and day,
and rises to song as blue as the sky abode,
as red as the paths of breath and the paths of blood,
as white as the moon, green as the living food.

Though stones may turn to lava, the trail remains—
a way across, from man to beast, and back.

Stream

I sit down beside her,
stream that carries me
to another corner of time.
She carries my separate longing
as I become another,
as paths of water carve their way
along my body,
beneath this mountain
and far beyond.

Resting in the slope shadow,
I become Stream
carrying myself along.
I cannot be hard for war.
I cannot be hard for love.
I am spirit warm to the touch
in this place of dawning miracles,
beneath this mountain
and far beyond.

Yesterday, now, and tomorrow
hold the shape of a single moment,
and the moment stalks my spirit.
Soon to be a mighty river, I
sit beside myself, spangled stream
that prances to a beckoning valley,
through rippling hills of moment,
beneath this mountain
and far beyond.

The Dreamcatcher

Old man on the Great Plains,
Once a warrior now a child,
Toys with a willow hoop—
And the Great Teacher Iktomi,
Now the Spider Iktomi,
Approaches with a purpose
Under Heaven.

And he speaks, as a spider
Might speak who would teach us
About cycles and passings—
From the infant to the child,
From the adult to the elder,
From the elder to the infant,
And beyond.

And he fills the willow circle
With his web, spinning words
About good things and bad—
How at each stage of life
There are right paths and wrong,
And a right choice to follow,
The Great Spirit.

With your face to the Creator
The web of life will carry
Your good dreams along—
And the nightmares that burn up
Can no longer hurt you.
For the children, make good use
Of your dreams.

The Eagle and The Condor

Delivered to the heights,
the Eagle spreads his wings,
soars on high to mark his prey
and astound with earthly force.

> Delivered to the heights,
> the Condor spreads her wings,
> conjures wonder in magic circles
> that embrace all lands and shores.

Patrolling acrobat,
he feasts in plundering haste,
among competing predators,
foragers, and feeders.

> Caring, nursing mother,
> she welcomes tomorrow-souls,
> amid incantations of holy priests,
> soothsayers, and seers.

He is mind and courage and industry;
and titan wings caress the wind
to stoke the fiery ritual of combat
unfettered.

> She is heart and earth and passion;
> and titan wings will not be folded
> till all mankind can see the dawn depart
> together.

> Beyond our time of healing and transformation
> when the Eagle and the Condor fly as one
> where the dawn is more than light
> every human step unveils
> a prophecy of change
> that leaves behind
> this waking
> dream

.

The Great Flood

In the First Creation, the Spirit Beings
Rock and Fire, Wind and Water,
were Powers to help the Creator, Powers
to make Earth and Moon, Sun and Stars—
Creation, woven to a harmony of laws,
in circles of birth and growth and death,
a gift of the One Great Spirit, Creator,
whose laws spin the workings of Powers and Beings.

When Grandmother Moon grew lonely in the dark,
Grandfather Thunder was given to Earth,
and through them humankind was conceived
of Moon and of Thunder, the last of Creation.
When Grandmother Moon was delivered unto spirit
her body remained to guide and to watch,
a sign of lasting love, lighting paths,
a sign of lasting faith, lighting dreams.

> But there came a time of blood and corruption—
> the corruption of violence fouling the Earth—

And the giant toad called the Water Keeper,
who could start and stop the rains with his will,
quarreled then battled with the covetous Serpent,
with the Hornèd Serpent jealous of waters.
Fury shook Earth and Sky, and their blood
spilled beneath winds rending heavens and seas.
But when Serpent slew Keeper, Creator sent Thunder's own
arrows of lightning to temper the storm.

The waters rose, and a Father of Man
called Nanapush sought to rise above
the raging currents that swallowed the Earth.
Nanapush, the Pure and Strong,
bounded up to the tallest peak,
scaled the heights with a silent cry
that summoned all creatures; eyes white with terror,
they climbed and climbed, as the waters rose.

And Nanapush sang above the torrents—
sang to a lone cedar tree at the summit—

The tree, filled with longing, reached through the mists,
grew, that all creatures might climb it together.
But as Nanapush nestled and prodded them on,
he grew tired of singing over careless wild forces,
over warrior forces howling all round.
So he tucked small branches under his belt,
then cast the branches onto the water.
And powers of spirit fashioned a raft.

Upon this largest and strongest of rafts,
Nanapush and all of his creatures were saved.

With waters at peace, he sent four creatures
far below to raise soil from the depths
of a world submerged in dark oblivion,
to plant the seed of the Old in the New.
Loon and Otter and Beaver returned
floating lifeless to the waves, and were reborn;
only Muskrat found earth, and so was promised
to rise eternal, through hate and scorn.

After the Flood

Pools of life, as the waters subside,
Carry cells of a reborn kind—

A sprout arises beyond its nature
Bearing Man, the Lonely Savior—

Lovely and pale, the willow tree
Bends to search for the unseen—

Where willow bows to kiss the earth,
Woman ascends, of shimmering birth—

Garden creatures tend to their needs,
Dance of the butterfly, honey of bees—

Song of the bird, milk of the beast,
Only the dog must wait till they sleep—

With little to offer, he lays at their side
His own gift of love for humankind.

The Handsome Weaver

Hanging in the room, beneath the gray adobe,
the Handsome Weaver's loom wove *mantas* for the lovely
women of the *pueblo*.
> *Shú-nah, shú-nah—Find her, find her—*
> *There—and away.*

Opulent his life, a dipping-gourd of pearl,
yet no wish to take a wife; he loved them all that were
the women of the *pueblo*.
> *Shú-nah, shú-nah—Find her.*

Coy the dimpled maidens that passed his door each day,
their gifts of buckskin laden with dancing fringe that sang,
> *See how we will love you.*
> *Shú-nah!*

And the tender Maiden Moon guarded dreams of the Handsome Weaver;
her one-eyed beauty shone thru the quiet love within her
for the Weaver of the *pueblo*.
> *Find her! Shú-nah!*

For her gift of food, he loved her,
but as passions brewed, they shunned her,
the Corn-Maidens of the Evil Road,
> *You are she—*
> *you are she.*

Come see your beauty! —with smiles that fell,
they beckoned the Moon to a watery well,
and admiring her own grace,
> she drowned
> *There—and away.*

And the Weaver sought his bride, beyond the gray adobe—
His mournful magic cried, *Return, return O Lovely*
Moon, or the pueblo will die!
> *Shú-nah, shú-nah! Find her!*
> *Aí-ay-ay, aí-ay-ay!*
> *There—*
> *and away.*

The Hunter

Autumn blood upon the leaf
flames among the burnished gold,
ascends to an azure heaven tossing
wisps of cloud on the water's face.

A feathered hunter plies the current,
paddles to the beat of a warrior's drum
that he alone is able to hear,
that softly echoes between heart and hand.

Now, again in the circle of time,
the sacred hunting ground will rise
above the riverbank, its treasures
promised for spring and the journey home—
        a hunter's wealth of meat and skins
        promised for the journey home.

———

Winter's solitary snows
fold about the hunter's camp,
awaken longings for a companion
against the dark and icy cold.

Suddenly magic comes to dwell—
beside a gentle smoldering fire
an unexpected gift, at close
of day, to please the tired hunter.

Supper in the bowl, garnished with love,
meat hung to dry and skins set for tanning.
Yet nowhere in the clean-swept lodge
is there a soul to thank for kindness—

        all prepared and served, cleaned and swept,
        but not a soul to thank.

———

Still memories prey on the hunter's mind—
a smile that has never been seen or exchanged,
a memory of silence never felt, never shared,
a touch recalled, but never bestowed.

Six days of magic, till on the seventh
animal tracks have been pressed in the snow,
where a trail tells the passing of the gentlest doe
and a feeling of loss returned to the woods.

Standing, eyes transfixing the trail,
the hunter looks on as bright colors fade,
until eyes and ears are reborn to change,
and all that remains are the deepest traces

        of a great stag running after his doe.
        And the bravest of hunters
        has vanished.

The Lover

When I see my love,
as constant as the rocks that we have climbed
to our mountaintop,
I remember how still we laughed at playful lights
in the northern sky.

As I watch my love,
I bid the eternal spirit of the wind
carry my song,
to celebrate in feathered dance and flight
all there is to say.

When I know my love
to be longing for the whirlwind's changing power,
I find dust to scatter,
and I challenge the snowy earth or the driving rain
for I too am whirlwind.

But to live in truth
is to find control in song between knowing smiles,
as the rest we take
from our struggle can turn the mountain and our bodies
into shards of light.

When I see my love,
I begin to speak in the dappled words of the river path.
But no one must see
how soft I have become, for surely to all
I must seem to forget

the rocks and the mountain,
the whirlwind and its tears of thirst and hunger,
and our blanket
of the deepest red that we have cinched with the whitest light.
But I haven't forgotten.
        I couldn't—when I see my love.

The Poet

I will speak,
for all to remember,
a breath of words—

words that echo
from love to war
war to love,
words that fight,
words that caress
the forms of a
man's own song,
words that beat and grind
against the stone
of a woman's song,
in a state of spirit and mind
arising.

In the fawn-eyed forest,
I find a song of dew
on my lips,
and flowers tossed at the moon.

I gaze out across the mesa,
and find a song
of painted ribbons
of earth and sky
that call to beloved beasts,
in the voices of rain and thunder.

Over the prairie grass,
I find a song
of flowing light and wind
and a call to the hunt.

I gaze out above the high summits,
and find a song
of heaven's high-born canyons
that spill sky and mist
to the valleys below—

and through it all

I repeat,
and repeat,
hallowed sounds that are true,
hallowed sounds that are truest
in their dance beneath the darkest
of clouds.

The Sacred Pipe

Wakan Chanunpa

Woman—
bring the Sacred Pipe.
Unwrap your bundle of finest skins
that shed their tones of forest and blood,
and open to the fire-warmed ground.

Red stone—
become the pipe's smooth bowl,
eternal color of womanly strength,
blood of ancients, grace the manly
pipe-stem tree of life.

Heaven—
join with Earth inviolate
as we take up the Sacred Pipe,
stumbling to rise and walk in prayer
as we bear our joy and grief.

But what
of the dark cloud sent to summon
the dour horizon of wounded souls,
or the blackened remains of wailing children—
what of the praised black cloud?

And why
are we ever lost to an Earth
that offers no garden free for the taking,
never failing to strafe its own paradise
in the heralded battle to be?

> *There is*
> *no need to wallow in grief,*
> *for those who bear the Sacred Pipe,*
> *for those who learn to walk in prayer,*
> *must know that all is Given.*

But then,
are we given this taste of Heaven
to temper the blackness of the cloud,
or are we given the blackest cloud
to temper our glimpse of Heaven?

> *There is*
> *no need to wallow in doubt,*
> *for those who bear the Sacred Pipe,*
> *for those who learn to walk in prayer,*
> *must know that All is given.*

The Town Crier

All awaken to the Town Crier's voice;
his call brings the sun to the moon.
Beneath clear eyes
or a clouded brow,
his lively summons cries,
Urgent! What has come!
What will come! What is now
come to be!

Here—
an eagle-message has fallen
through abundant signs of the season:
Rejoice in the rains, and if snows are but kind
all needs will be provided!

There—
a call-to-hunt storms the prairie
and all fields that carry the sky.
Come, make arrows, come!
The buffalo rises and bounty springs
from deep in the earth once again!

And the Crier's firm steps
among chiefs and high priests
bring ritual to the realm of cause and effect,
bring order to the land of the Peaceful People,
bring tidings to the village of souls.

But then—
among walls of adobe or of buffalo skin,
of wattle and daub or of glass and steel,
who will heed the freely cried news
of the Crier?

Where there is Village, there are those
who will listen and act in harmony.
Where there is Suspicion, there are those
who will listen and act in disharmony.
Where there is Resentment, there are those
who will rejoice in the failure of others.
Where there is Enmity, there are those
who will act to destroy and undo.
Where there is Fear, there are those
who will scamper, to share the news.
Where there is Sloth, there are those
who will push on through a turbid sea.

All awaken to the Town Crier's voice,
for his call brings the sun to the moon.

The White Buffalo

Two men walk the savage trail of heat and famine.
They hunt for food where only hope can find them.
Their wooded path is bowered and draped in cloud and mist
as if the Heavens above and Earth below would guide them
to a carnal feast, on the savage trail of heat and famine.

A conjuring cloud now molds the roiling mist to fantasy.
Woman-form breathes life from lines and swirls.
White buckskin grace that floats to walk, she steps more softly
than the mist, feels the hunters' hope, and turns
to cast the beauty of her gaze, calling the mist to fantasy.

The first hunter lowers his eyes; he knows *Wakan*: the Sacred.
The second, caught in lust and raw desire,
awakens a mother's heart that loves her children wisely,
yet awakens a woman's wrath at lustful fire.
She beckons, bids him approach *Wakan*: the Sacred.

And as he approaches, a tower of dust and ash arises
to hide the Sacred and the base profane from view.
When the dust has settled, a mound of bones stand by her.
She has but given the wanton soul his due—
a moment's lifetime of lust where the tower of ash arises.

The first hunter's virtue still rests upon the trail,
wanting to heal the lifeless path between them.
And through the virtuous hunter, she offers to his people
a sacred pipe that he might share among them—
with Seven Prayers, before the Sins and Wonders on the trail.

—*Return to your people, tell them I am coming*—
And as she leaves, she turns and turns again,
each time she paints the colors of humankind, until at last
she stands, white bison of the plains, White Buffalo Woman,
against the darkest times, an omen and a promise:
—*Return to your people, and tell them I am coming.*

About the Author

Cary Kamarat is a native of Chicago and alumnus of Northwestern University's School of Communication. He has taught at Evergreen State College in Washington State and NATO Defense College in Rome. His poetry has appeared in *The Federal Poet*, *Poets on the Fringe*, *Prospectus: A Literary Offering*, and the *District Lines Anthology*. He has also been published online at *Academic Exchange Quarterly*, *First People: Native American Poems and Prayers*, and *Israel National Radio*. His photography has appeared in *The Tulane Review* and *District Lines*; and his online travel articles and photos have reached a broad international audience. His debut collection, *Travelwalk: Poems and Images*, was published in 2014 followed by *Out of Delmarva* in 2015. Now a resident of Maryland's Eastern Shore, he has continued to read his own poetry at several venues in the Washington DC area, in Chicago, and on the Shore.